[COVER PAGE]

Mine *Their* Business

Generation Z

Timeless principles for maintaining a successful business

Abijah Duran

Contents

Introduction

If you're reading this to learn how to start a business, you're in the wrong place. This write-up is for millennials and the denizens of Generation Z who've already set up a business and are now wrestling with the not-so-easy task of maintaining it. In short, this book doesn't aim to teach you how to start a business, rather it teaches you how to mind your business, or in much better terms, mind *their* business, because you may be running the business but it also belongs to all of your customers, employees, and vendors.

This phrase might sound similar to 'mind your own business.' But the omission of 'own' makes all the difference. This is because, in the business world, you cannot simply mind your own business; you must also keep an eye on your rival's business in order to stay relevant and competitive, and you must take into consideration how all the people that are connected to your business feel about it.

In 2016, there were more than 25 million Americans running their own business [1]. More and more people are encouraged to start their own ventures than ever before. They are mesmerized by the idea of being their own boss: not answerable to anybody, ordering people around, coming and going as they please and making piles of money while doing it.

The reality is far less rosy. Truth is that while establishing a business is hard enough, keeping a business running is even harder. It requires you to work long hours, sacrifice sleep, personal life, vacations and hobbies. You have to constantly monitor every team working under you. Unless you've completely self-financed your business, which is rare, you're also going to be answerable to investors and other stakeholders. In short, the hard part of entrepreneurship doesn't end when your business generates its first profit; it only gets harder.

Regardless, having your own business does have its kicks. Employees who decide to make the switch and become independent employers feel more fulfilled and motivated to work. It gives you the freedom to experiment that creative, ambitious people need. But at the end of the day, if the numbers don't add up, it can all come crashing down.

How do you stop that from happening? How do you ensure that your business has all the ingredients to move beyond a lucky startup to something more long lasting and stable? These are difficult questions.

Let's start answering them.

Principle #1: Forming Strong Business Relationships

While being attentive to your business is easily done (it is your business after all) many young entrepreneurs don't recognize the importance of business relationships, and if they do, they're usually not willing to invest the time and effort necessary to foster them. They solely focus on improving their product, believing that if their product is top-notch there's no way it could fail.

This approach is problematic. You may think that the only type of relationship you should have with people in your business is one in which money exchanges hands and conversations are full of work jargon. This is what a basic work relationship is. Going beyond this baseline and cultivating more human, personal relationships can open up opportunities that you may never have thought of.

Although the list can expand depending on what sort of business you're in, there are four essential business relationships:

- Vendors
- Employees
- Customers
- Industry partners/colleagues

Let's look at several ways you can start creating more fruitful business relationships:

- **Start diversifying your networks:** Being in the car rental service doesn't mean your network should begin and end on car dealers. Try to make connections in other industries as well, even if they don't directly relate to your company's market. Knowing what other industries are up to can lead to new ideas, collaborations, and other opportunities beneficial for your business. For instance, the owner of a car rental service could meet someone from the restaurant industry and realize they can collaborate on a food delivery service. These sort of ideas are only possible if you know people in sectors as diverse as heavy industry, software, media and government.
    - Attend conferences, industry meetups to meet the leaders and newcomers in your field.
    - Extend a simple lunch invite to potential connections. Get to know them, where they're from, what they like. You may talk a little business with them as well, but it's better to establish personal rapport before doing so.
    - When expanding your network, the best place to start is the community that you are based in or are marketing your business to. Getting to know their values, their aspirations, and needs will allow you to serve them better and thus foster mutual respect and trust.
- **Show what you can do for them:** 'Serving is the new selling' sums up the trend in the business landscape today. You have to show what you can do for people to make them warm up to you. This applies to communities you want to work with as

well. Fund charities, host seminars, publish articles, give your insights. Add value to peoples' lives and they will reciprocate by giving you their trust and bringing value to your business.

- o Remember to only invest as much into a relationship as you plan to get out of it. Unless you have personal, emotional reasons to invest in a particular activity such as charity or helping marginalized communities, don't go out of your way to become friends with a business partner if you know they can't reciprocate your effort with tangible benefits.
- o Have zero expectations. Don't assume anything. Remember the golden rule: Lesser the expectations, lesser the disappointment.
- **Find common ground:** It's easier to form relationships with individuals and companies whose values and aims align with yours. If you're aiming to make environmentally friendly shampoo bottles seek out organizations that value sustainability. If you're passionate about helping kids, get in touch with individuals who are doing just that in their communities.

There are other things you can do to nurture your work relationships. Find out what strategies suit your personality and circumstances. But keep in mind that there is no such thing as a solopreneur. All businesses need to maintain mutually beneficial relationships with suppliers, investors, customers, employees and any other stakeholders. The most long-lasting relationships are always the ones based on authenticity, respect and commonality.

Principle #2: Treating Your Employees Right

Michael Monteiro, CEO of Buildium (a growing property management software company out of Boston) believes that to build a successful company culture, you have to answer three core questions:

- Why does our company do what it does (i.e. Why do we exist)?
- What do we believe (i.e. what are our values)?
- Where do we want to go with the company (i.e. what is our vision for the company)? [2]

Company culture is the personality of the company. A study from Glassdoor found that 65% of millennials look at a company's culture before they apply compared to 52% of people who are 45 or older. Needless to say, this trend will continue to rise as more and more young people join the job market. Therefore, in order to inspire loyalty, creativity and productivity in your current employees and attract the most suitable talent later on, you must define your company culture early on. Defining a culture from scratch is always easier than changing a culture that is ingrained.

The reason we've talked about culture in some detail above is because it defines how your team managers deal with their employees, how your employees behave with each other, and finally, how everyone in the company perceives you. Since you're the founder of the company, the company's culture can be what you want it to be. In general, this should be a culture based on transparency, respect, empathy, and a common purpose.

Make a personal connection: Get to know your team. Organize monthly luncheons with them. Inquire after their wellbeing and that of their families. Make it a point to know everyone's names as quickly as you can. Managers that are cold, distant or aloof also appear untrustworthy and unlikeable, and this can discourage people working under you.

Don't command, but encourage: As we've mentioned above, people don't like being told how to do their job. Rather than command your workers to do something a certain way, encourage them to do it that way. Show your employees that your goals, your company's goals, and their goals are all aligned. This is easier to do when you've hired people who believe in the company's culture from the start.

So define your expectations and the criteria by which you will judge performance, and give your employees the autonomy to do things their way.

No nepotism: This is the biggest mistake you could absolutely make. Never, ever have favorites in your team. Other people are quick to catch nepotism and it will destroy your credibility, integrity and respect amongst your staff. Establish a set of rules by which you will evaluate employee performance. Write down SOPs for how to deal with a difficult team member and apply them equally to everyone.

Model the behavior you seek: This last piece of advice encompasses pretty much everything said above. 'Treat others as you would like to be treated.' If you want your employees to be tolerant of each other, empathetic to one another, kind and caring, you must demonstrate all these qualities in the way you personally behave with them. This means not losing your temper when they make mistakes, understanding and supporting them when tragedy strikes, and being easily accessible to all of them.

We will now look at an example of how a proactive CEO can redefine a company's culture even in times of crisis.

United Way of the North Carolinas is a non − profit organization that focuses on education, health and basic needs. In 2009, it was awash with scandals about mismanagement and overly-generous executive salary packages. Donations to the organization had been reduced to a trickle, and employees were angry and felt betrayed. The financial crisis hit during this time as well, prompting layoffs and cost cutting.

It was this mess that Jane McIntyre inherited when she became CEO. She knew she had to earn the trust of her employees quickly and redefine company culture. This is what she did on her very first staff welcome:

As the staff assembled to welcome her, someone asked her what her first priority was going to be. "There was this glass door that had been installed between the lobby and the executive offices," McIntyre says. "The door was always shut. So I said, you see that door? It's never going to close. And the staff burst into applause."

Though Jane had to make difficult cuts in the months to come, she made sure that every decision was delivered with candor and honesty. She created compulsory all-staff meetings because she felt she "had to communicate face to face" with employees, especially when it came to delivering difficult news.

She made accessibility her hallmark. She says that while it may slow you down, it pays off enormously in the long-run if you're trying to create a friendly work culture.

Today, the organization is exceeding its fundraising goals and increasing grants to local charitable agencies. But Jane sees the progress she's made in earning employees' trust most clearly in the tenor of the all-staff meetings. "When I started, it was like you were in a graveyard," she says. "There were no questions, no expressions. Now people laugh, they cut up, they have fun. There is camaraderie." [3]

Defining a company culture based on trust, transparency, respect between employer and employee and empathy can thus lead to a stronger company that is more capable of surviving in hard times as well as thriving in good times.

Principle #3: The Customer is the Lifeline of Your Business

Customer satisfaction depends on a product's performance against the customers' expectations. If the product performs below expectations the customer is dissatisfied and vice versa.

Studies show that greater customer satisfaction leads to greater customer loyalty, with some customers becoming stringent supporters of the company and advertising it via word of mouth. In general, higher customer satisfaction correlates to greater company success.

This section will be different from the ones above. Here we're going to focus more on citing examples from contemporary as well as early companies on how to satisfy, attract and value the people who keep your proverbial wheels spinning: your customers.

Who is a customer?

L.L Bean is in the top 10 of every list of the best service companies. The outdoor apparel maker was founded in 1912, but when asked "What is a customer?" its founder Leon Leonwood Bean responded with this timeless answer:

"A customer is the most important person ever in this company—in person or by mail. A customer is not dependent on us, we are dependent on him. A customer is not an interruption of our work, he is the purpose of it. We are not doing a favor by serving him, he is doing us a favor by giving us the opportunity to do so. A customer is not someone to argue or match wits with. Nobody ever won an argument with a customer. A customer is a

person who brings us his wants. It is our job to handle them profitably to him and to ourselves."

Even a hundred years later, the founder's words still define the company's culture and treatment of its customers.

Is aweing customers necessary?

One misconception when it comes to customer care is that customers need to be pampered and showered with attention in order to win their support. This isn't necessarily true, as German grocery chain ALDI proves:

ALDI has highly satisfied customers, even though they have to bag their own groceries and can't use credit cards. ALDI's everyday very low pricing on good-quality products delights customers and keeps them coming back. Thus, customer satisfaction comes not just from service heroics but from how well a company delivers on its basic value proposition and helps customers solve their buying problems.

"Most customers don't want to be 'wowed,'" says one marketing consultant. "They [just] want an effortless experience."

Know your customers

Involvement of CEOs and executives can also play their role in bringing customers on board. Take the example of Target's energetic CEO, Brian Cornell:

Brian likes nosing around stores and getting a real feel for what's going on. It gives him "great, genuine feedback." He and other Target executives even visit customers in their homes, opening closet doors and poking around in cupboards to understand their product choices and buying habits.

Similarly, Boston Market CEO George Michel makes frequent visits to company restaurants, working in the dining room and engaging customers to learn about "the good, the bad, and the ugly." He also stays connected by reading customer messages on the Boston Market website and has even cold-called customers for insights. "Being close to the customer is critically important," says Michel. "I get to learn what they value, what they appreciate."

Be more than just a product

The best way to retain customer loyalty is not to offer people just a product, or just a solution, but rather give them an all-encompassing experience. This is demonstrated by Buffalo Wild Wings.

While the fast growing restaurant chain offers great selection of wings and beer, and people love gobbling them up (the chain sold 11 million wings across the United States on Super Bowl Sunday alone), the key ingredient is not simply good food, rather it's the experience. People come to B-Dubs to watch sports, trash talk, cheer on their sports teams, and meet old friends and make new ones—that is, a total eating and social experience.

"We realize that we're not just in the business of selling wings," says the company. "We're something much bigger. We're in the business of fueling the sports fan experience. Our mission is to WOW people every day!"

In short then, a company should incorporate quality customer service as a policy, not as an afterthought or hassle. This service doesn't have to be fancy, but it should make the customer feel valued, heard and appreciated [4].

Principle #4: Financial Transparency

A survey conducted by Robert Half, a recruiting firm, revealed some interesting facts.

- 82% of workers want updates on company financial performance.
- 87% of CFOs at these organizations said quarterly and annual information is made available to at least select employees, up 31 points from a similar survey in 2016.
- 56% of companies in the survey give updates to all workers [5].

What this means is that there's a trend towards more and more financial transparency in organizations. Younger workers in particular demand it and it boosts customer confidence as well.

Buffer is a company that embraces transparency in its core values. The social media scheduling company has made the salaries of its employees public in a Google doc. Everyone from the CEO to the most junior employee's salary is listed there. Not only that, it also makes the formula by which the salary is calculated public as well. This communicates a level of fairness and avoids employee bitterness in salary differences, while also boosting trust in the company.

A touring and vendor access company called Zapper has also incorporated transparency into its DNA. This is exemplified by an entire department in the organization called Zappos Insights, which facilitates tours of the Zappos headquarters and live training events. Attendees can even schedule Q&A sessions with specific departments within Zappos, including customer service, user experience, and marketing.

A word of caution

While these companies have managed to use financial and operational transparency in their favor, it is better for a company to carefully evaluate how transparent it should be with its employees and the public. To do this, you should keep the basic objective of your company in mind:

- Improve its performance by attracting more customers and retaining existing ones.
- Give its employees a better standard of living [6]

If you feel being financially transparent can help you achieve those goals, then go ahead. But if it does not it will, be cautious. In some cases, salary sharing can fuel dissent and fighting amongst employees. Sometimes providing company statistics to employees who don't need to know them can distract or overwhelm them.

Still, transparency is not a fad. It is a trend that will turn into a norm in the coming years. If you're a young company, it is worth considering it.

Principle #5: You Do Not Run the Show

Most of this guide has been focused on telling you what to do, how to do, and when to do it. This section in the end is supposed to remind you that it's *not all about you.*

Entrepreneurs by nature are dynamic people. They're willing to take risks, they're visionary, they're ambitious. These are all admirable qualities and any person embodying them will find it easier to get a business up and running than someone without them.

Do not be selfish

However, once a company is established, this same mindset may lead to problems. Many entrepreneurs tie their personal wealth to the business. This is fine, but it often leads to the entrepreneur pushing the business to expand when it can't support doing so, or cutting down employees to increase profits.

At other times, the cocky CEO, inspired by his business doing well, starts to indulge in all sorts of excesses. These excesses eventually turn into debt that revenue from the business fails to pay off, and the company goes bankrupt.

This kind of cavalier attitude often compromises the business ecosystem which helped establish the business in the first place. This eco system is made up of vendors, legal experts, industry rivals, employees and customers. If you don't keep the interests of these people in your mind in every business decision, they will lose trust in you and won't give you their support on your next venture.

The point of reiterating all of this is to stress that ego or a sense of superiority will not get you far in today's business landscape. Back in the old times people either had to work in farms or factories and the people they worked under were cut from the same cloth. Today, the choices of workplace available to people are immense and they will always opt for the company that's about something bigger than one person, that makes them feel heard and values them.

Be that company.

Avoid micro-managing

Another mistake entrepreneurs often make is trying to micro-manage all the teams under them. There's nothing wrong in being aware of all your business interests and actively involved in the work being done by your teams. In the early days of your business, employees are looking to you for guidance, inspiration, and direction.

This doesn't mean that you start telling them how to do their job though. You hired these people because they have more expertise in a particular function of business (like finances, legal, marketing etc.) than you do. You should respect their intellect and give them the space to pursue the company's objectives their way. Too much interference risks annoying your employees or discouraging them from taking initiatives by themselves.

Empower your team

Let's look at Mike Volpe. Chief Marketing Officer of a software company called Hubspot. Mike's company was expanding at a tremendous pace. He went from managing 20 people to 50 in about nine months. He was finding it hard to remember everyone's names and connect with them.

One thing Mike did do though was give his marketing department tremendous autonomy. Here's what he had to say about that:

"When you manage 15 or 20 people, you can be that person who approves things before they go out," he says. *"But once we started to grow quickly, I became a giant bottleneck. I knew I needed to trust the team to get things out. And we found the employees do a better job when you give them that authority and responsibility."* [3]

Another generic example is that of your vendor/supplier. You may think they're just interested in sales, but put yourself in their shoes for one second and think: Who would you offer a better deal to? An up and coming capitalist who growls and treats you as little more than a means to achieve his ends? Or a humble, friendly entrepreneur that realizes that you and he are not all that different? The answer is as clear as day. Having a good relationship with your vendor allows your business to get the products or services it needs faster, save money and give it a competitive edge in the marketplace.

So then, while you should be proactive in running your business and realize that your role is crucial in moving the company forward, do not fall into the trap of thinking that it was all because of you. Your associates, be they employees, clients, investors, vendors, community leaders, had a big role to play in your success. Don't forget them when you succeed and they'll continue to help you achieve future goals as well.

Long story short: stay humble.

Conclusion

We started by saying that keeping a business running after you've established it is not easy. We then talked about how important it is to nurture and foster strong, reliable relationships with your business ecosystem. We then looked into how you should define your company culture, its importance, and what that culture should look like. Then we talked about customers and their importance for your business and why should always place their needs above yours. Then we looked at financial transparency, with both internal and external shareholders and why it may be beneficial for your company. Finally, we addressed the need to not let success go to your head and to remain mindful of the people around you.

While a lot of this advice can vary from person to person, you should carefully evaluate it in the unique context of your business environment. The general idea it seeks to communicate is more or less the same no matter where you are: business is not business as usual. It is unusual and nearly impossible for it to thrive in this generation without transparency, accountability, respect and love.

References

[1] [Online]. Available:
    https://www.freshbooks.com/press/annualreport.

[2] [Online]. Available: https://business.linkedin.com/talent-
    solutions/blog/company-culture/2018/build-company-
    culture-small-business.

[3] [Online]. Available: https://hbr.org/2014/06/proven-ways-to-earn-
    your-employees-trust.

[4] P. Kotler, Principles of Marketing.

[5] [Online]. Available: http://rh-us.mediaroom.com/2020-01-28-
    Survey-82-Of-Workers-Want-Updates-On-Company-Financial-
    Performance.

[6] [Online]. Available:
    https://www.forbes.com/sites/fotschcase/2017/01/24/using-
    transparency-to-build-a-better-company/#56fc434e72c6.

Special Thanks......

Special Thanks to Friends, Family & Mentors!

Last but never least, I Thank GOD!

For giving me talents and treasures beyond my expectation or imagination. I'm so truly thankful for his many blessings and what he has done and continues to do for ALL.

GOD is awesome and amazingly the best experience, the best gift that is forever unmatched. To GOD be the glory!

www.ingramcontent.com/pod-product-compliance
Lightning Source LLC
Chambersburg PA
CBHW031512210526
45463CB00008B/3204